Marking the Millennium

THE CELEBRATION OF A LIFETIME
AT THE WALT DISNEY WORLD® RESORT

TEXT BY PAM BRANDON

DISNEP

EDITIONS

Photography on pgs. 1, 3, 50, 55, 58, 59, 60, 61, 68, 69 © Robert Desmond
Photography on pgs. 56, 57 © Don Dorsey
For Disney Editions
Editor: Wendy Lefkon
Assistant Editor: Rich Thomas

For Roundtable Press, Inc.
Directors: Susan E. Meyer, Marsha Melnick, Julie Merberg
Editor: John Glenn
Project Coordinator, Computer Production, Photo Editor, Designer: Steven Rosen

ISBN 0-7868-6605-5

First Edition
2   4   6   8   10   9   7   5   3   1

Marking the Millennium

THE CELEBRATION OF A LIFETIME AT THE WALT DISNEY WORLD® RESORT

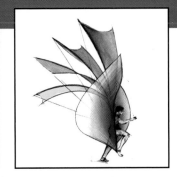

The clock is ticking . . . and whether you believe the dawn of the new century begins January 1, 2000, or January 1, 2001, only one place on earth is actually celebrating the new millennium every single day for fifteen months—Epcot® at Walt Disney World® Resort.

Epcot, an acronym coined by Walt Disney in 1966 meaning Experimental Prototype Community of Tomorrow, was envisioned as a "living blueprint of the future," a place where guests could come to learn about the world around them and discover the challenges of tomorrow. Comprised of Future World and World Showcase, the discovery park offers a blend of technology and world cultures. "Epcot appeals most to the explorer in all of us, that part that is curious about people, places, and progress in the real world," says George Kalogridis, vice president for Epcot.

For The Walt Disney Company, the international leader in entertainment, one New Year's Eve was simply not enough to mark a historic milestone that happens only once every fifty generations. In true Disney fashion, Walt Disney World Resort is marking the millennium every day from October 1, 1999, through January 1, 2001. The goal for the dream makers at Walt Disney Imagineering and Walt Disney World Creative Entertainment is to create the most extraordinary celebration in the world, "an international celebration of the human spirit, showcasing the accomplishments of today that will shape our world tomorrow."

With the theme "Celebrate the Future Hand in Hand," the Epcot fête is both magnificent and emotional, a memorable way to cross the threshold into the new century.

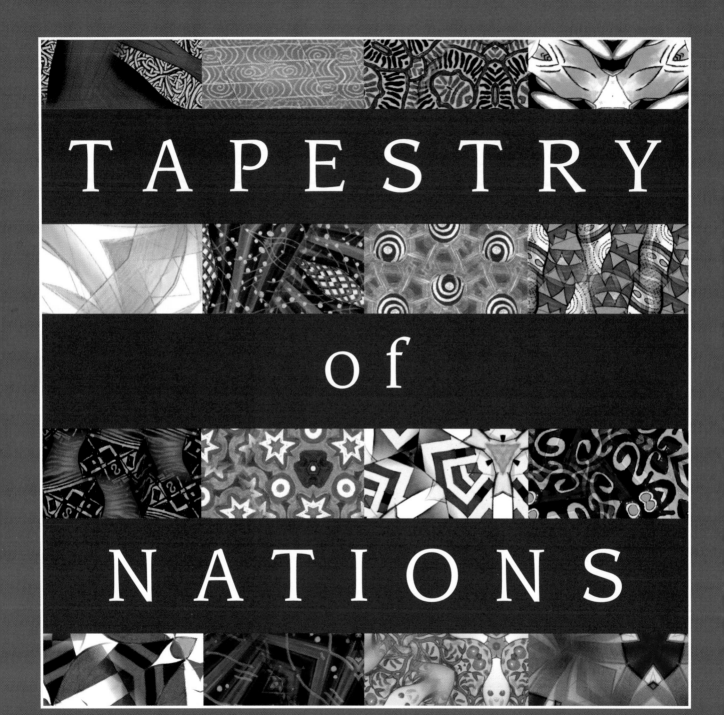

TAPESTRY
of
NATIONS

he gateway of time has opened and the spirit of humanity has brought us together. Let us reach out and touch. Peace and goodwill to all who gather here for this earthly celebration. May the spirit of humanity bring us together . . . may the promise of the new millennium light the child within your heart. And now . . . as the millennium drums unite and become one heartbeat, let us fly together hand in hand on the wings of joy, kindness, compassion, and love.

— From the opening for
Tapestry of Nations

Bold and vibrant bits and pieces from Michael Curry's drawings of the puppets in *Tapestry of Nations*, opposite page, form their own tapestry of colors and patterns.

How do we celebrate the *world*?

This was the daunting, open-ended challenge Gary Paben, Walt Disney World® Entertainment show director for the Epcot® Millennium Celebration, posed to his creative team. Their ultimate solution was as extraordinary as it was ambitious: a fantastic, transnational vision of a tapestry.

"A tapestry has many threads, and our tapestry symbolically represents the diversity of planet Earth, and our hope for a better world woven with compassion, love, kindness, and joy," Paben explains. "When you weave all of these elements into it, you have a magnificent image, and that image represents the human spirit."

The Story Begins

HOW DO WE CELEBRATE THE WORLD?

Above, Gary Paben stands amidst models, storyboards, and drawings for *Tapestry of Nations*, the nightly spectacle celebrating the new millennium. Opposite page, larger-than-life figures adorned in vivid colors are the centerpiece of *Tapestry of Nations*. These enormous figures soar nearly 20 feet high and are controlled by performers dressed in elaborate costumes.

Tapestry of Nations, the nighttime spectacular created for the 15-month-long Epcot Millennium Celebration, celebrates the human spirit with enormous puppets spilling onto World Showcase Promenade, 150 performers interacting with guests, and thrilling music—all combining in a swirl of sights and sounds that immerses viewers in an entertaining and meaningful spectacular.

The Concept

Tapestry of Nations was a work in progress at Epcot® for three years—the longest development time ever for a Disney show. Show director Paben recalls that the first idea out of the box was a show called *Caravan of Giants* for World Showcase Promenade. But he kept searching for a theme for the millennium that would have "more soul and a signature of its own." The working title became *Millenium 2000,* then *Earth 2000,* then *Tapestry of Dreams.* Ultimately, it evolved into *Tapestry of Nations,* a name defining a celebration that would embrace an international audience. Paben's vision was to create a tribal experience that would be driven by the human heartbeat—drums—and would take the audience on a spiritual journey with larger-than-life puppets, an emotional score, and primitive flames of light.

The core team grew quickly. Paben, who has more than 20 years' experience of working on Disney extravaganzas, called on longtime associates to share his vision for the project. He felt that the all-embracing nature of the *Tapestry of Nations* called for many ideas and many people working together side by side. Early team members included choreographer Gail Davies-Siegler, Broadway lighting designer David Agress, puppet expert Michael Curry, set designer Lynn Holloway, costume designer Marilyn Sotto Erdmann, and composer Gavin Greenaway.

John Haupt, another Disney veteran, returned from Tokyo Disneyland® Resort to join the team as managing producer, "looking out for everything from A to Z, making sure everybody keeps moving in the same direction," as he describes it. "It's a balancing act between fiscal responsibility and creative intent."

> **"There had to be an emotional connection, something that guests could react to, something that touches them."**
>
> *John Haupt,*
> *Managing Producer*

The stilt-walking Sage of Time, opposite page, begins the dramatic procession around World Showcase Lagoon. His massive cloak is a brilliant amalgam of iridescent bronze, gold, and copper. Left, guests are encouraged to interact with the entertainers and the giant puppets as they make their way around the promenade. Above, the puppet known as Bird Man spreads its wings over World Showcase Promenade.

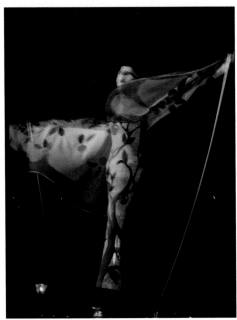

The *Tapestry of Nations* costumes add 15 to 18 feet to the height of performers, but to the guests, the puppetry appears simple and effortless as the performers dance their way around World Showcase Lagoon. The show is performed in two parts each evening, beginning at sunset, with a barrage of sights and sounds. The second performance occurs after dark, when the lighted costumes create an ethereal ambience.

Creative sessions began to focus on the millennium as a time of celebration, but also a time of introspection. "There had to be an emotional connection," insists Haupt, "something that guests could react to, something that would touch them deeply."

Essential elements were a storyteller, a unique backdrop, and a show with enough sheer visual density to create the party of a lifetime on the mile-long World Showcase Promenade. But *Tapestry of Nations* is not simply a parade of fanciful floats and marching musicians; it's an interactive procession that uses three basic components—light, music, and street performers—to take advantage of the Promenade's spaciousness. Fifteen huge rolling drum units, played by 30 live drummers, are the only set pieces.

The storyteller is the Sage of Time, "like a pied piper, a grandfatherly figure who starts the entire celebration," describes Paben. "His face is the sun, because the sun is familiar to all cultures, and his elaborate cloak is covered with timepieces that have been used by all cultures." Three Sages appear around

The puppeteers have fun with the crowds—there are no ropes to keep the guests from joining the procession, and a Carnivale atmosphere fills the World Showcase Promenade.

World Showcase Promenade suggesting that there is no beginning or end to the grand fête. While the Sage of Time, 120 giant puppets, and 30 drummers create a dazzling feast for the eyes, the music is always at the center of the extravaganza. Gavin Greenaway, the composer of the music for *Tapestry of Nations*, also scored *IllumiNations 2000: Reflections of Earth,* the fireworks and music spectacle that closes each night's festivities around the World Showcase Lagoon.

"The music is really the soul, the pulse of our celebration," enthuses Paben. "It is the soundtrack that takes you on a journey where you cannot stop dancing and rejoicing."

Greenaway's music for *Tapestry of Nations* influenced the creation of the ethereal puppets, the show's visual centerpiece. "I heard the musical score early on," recounts Michael Curry, the designer of the *Tapestry of Nations* puppets. "The music had a big symphonic sense as well as a percussive base, so I tried to stay with big, diaphanous, open structures, and suggest, at the same time, a real sense of kinetics, because behind the music you can feel this drumbeat, this highly percussive background."

The show is performed in two parts each evening, beginning at sunset with a barrage of sights and colors. "It's like looking at a living tapestry displaying the diversity of the human spirit, never seeing the same image twice," describes Paben. The second performance occurs after dark, with 19 fiery torches adding a theatrical backdrop. The show culminates as the theatrical lighting is lowered and moving mirrored surfaces at the top of the rolling percussion units are illuminated, creating a starry effect that washes over the entire promenade.

"The ultimate look of the show captures the art from the Louvre, the D'Orsay, The Metropolitan Museum of Art, and the British Museum, and crushes it into tiny pieces that are exploded inside a giant snow globe," explains Paben with a smile. "The fragments mix together to create the unity of the human spirit." That is his whimsical description to convey the look of *Tapestry of Nations*. "When you go to an art museum, you're looking at wonderful shapes and designs, and every piece of art means something different to every person."

The project's design goal was to suggest unity and connection. According to Curry, the team set out to create an overlay, or abstract notion of a Tapestry of Nations, that represents all

Designing the Dream

AT THE HEART OF IT ALL IS THE ARTIST

Michael Curry, above, at work on one of the *Tapestry of Nations* puppets in his studio in St. Helens, Oregon. Curry's color sketches, like the one on the opposite page, prepared the way for the elaborate costumes that were created for *Tapestry of Nations*.

cultures combined rather than a specific ethnic point of origin. What emerges is a composite of visual elements from around the world, created in a way that doesn't really give away their source.

Curry, winner of two Emmy Awards and a Tony Award for his design work on Disney's *The Lion King* on Broadway, is one of the country's leading puppet experts. Designing a show like *Tapestry of Nations* is, he says, more challenging than designing for the stage.

The first hurdle to clear, for example, was the sheer size of World Showcase Lagoon. It was difficult, Curry reports, to create a visual line around the entire lagoon substantial enough to warrant

a celebration for Epcot®. To achieve a sense of scale, Curry's team first created huge cardboard cutouts of the puppets and tested the look around the lagoon.

At the same time the puppets needed to make a striking impression from across the lagoon, so it was equally important that the spectacle be impressive in close quarters as well. Curry rose to the challenge: "I enjoy the absolute immediacy of an audience three feet away in broad daylight looking you in the eyes," he exclaims, "the sort of ancient quality of standing in the daylight and performing for an audience. There are no controls, no editing, filtering, adapting, coloring—it has to be good every time."

Curry's designs draw the audience in by having the puppeteers and the puppets viewable at the same time. In fact, Curry rarely hides the performer's interaction with the puppet. "People share a sense of complicity with the performance when they see both the puppet and the puppeteer," he explains. "It's like seeing two shows in one. Epcot is a perfect world for this sort of approach and people gravitate right to the eyes when they get close, identifying first with the performer."

The blending of creativity with functionality represented the biggest challenge in realizing the *Tapestry of Nations* puppets. The show's weather, maintenance, and engineering issues are unusual by theater standards. Because *Tapestry of Nations* will run every day for 15 months, the artful designs must withstand daily heat and humidity, ultraviolet degradation from sunlight, and the general wear and tear of the performers. "I try to think creatively first," Curry muses, "without being too restricted by the realities of functionality and engineering, but very quickly I fold these into the design. You have to be a composite engineer, a structural engineer, and something of a color theorist in order to accomplish this, but at the heart of it all is the artist."

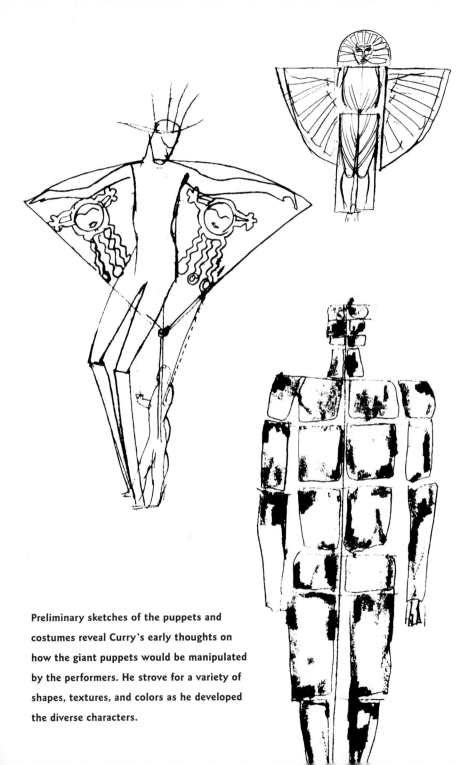

From the Beginning

"Like any artist, I work first with notions and feelings," describes Curry. He develops pencil sketches, called thumbnails, to start. "In the beginning I'm most concerned with silhouettes. I want to see the whole composition in a space." For *Tapestry of Nations,* Curry started with many silhouettes. Taken together, they had to connect visually while preserving "a variety of lines, textures, and colors at the same time."

Reflecting the transnational theme of Disney's Epcot® Millennium Celebration, the puppets are not specifically South American, African, or Asian, but are created with patterns, shapes, and colors that suggest many ethnicities. From the start, *Tapestry of Nations* expressed unity, permeating every creation through music, costuming, lighting, sound, puppetry, and direction. "What

Preliminary sketches of the puppets and costumes reveal Curry's early thoughts on how the giant puppets would be manipulated by the performers. He strove for a variety of shapes, textures, and colors as he developed the diverse characters.

I really hope to achieve at Epcot® is for you to feel a sense of unity with your neighbor, to feel a sense of uplifting joy in being with someone who happens to be of a different nationality."

Tapestry of Nations features 20-foot-tall aerial rod puppets that integrate the performer with the puppet. Curry named each one of the 120 puppets. For example, Bird Man has a bird's beak and plumage. Aztec Man features open netting, metal fabrics and hand-applied silver leaf, and wings that are a canvas for Curry's paintings. Inverted Marionette is a whimsical piece with a marionette controlling another puppet, a good example of a total body puppet controlled by the performer. Others have names like Angel Girl and Wiggle Girl, each with wings, capes, drapes, or sails in beautiful, sheer materials that let light pass through them. There are forty different styles of puppets in all, three of each design.

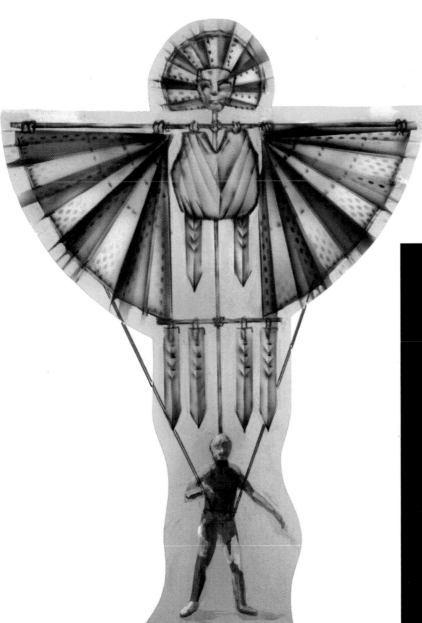

The brilliant colors and textures of Curry's creations are inspired by visual elements from around the world. Shown here are designs for Aztec Man, whose open wings are a resplendent canvas. Below, a miniature model of one of the designs for Aztec Man, painted with hand-applied silver leaf.

Variations on Bird Man come to life in Curry's drawings and in a miniature model, opposite page. Curry was inspired by the butterfly, and created a wrapped torso flanked by painted fabrics that emulate butterfly wings. The stylized beak and brilliant plumage of the headwear add a tribal look to the majestic structure, which is so lightweight that it appears to float above the costumed puppeteer.

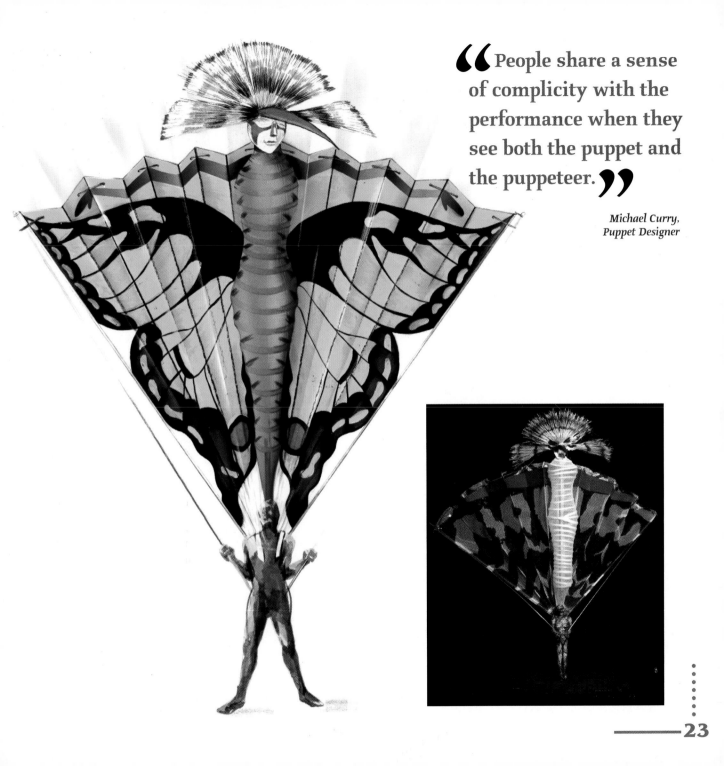

" People share a sense of complicity with the performance when they see both the puppet and the puppeteer. **"**

Michael Curry,
Puppet Designer

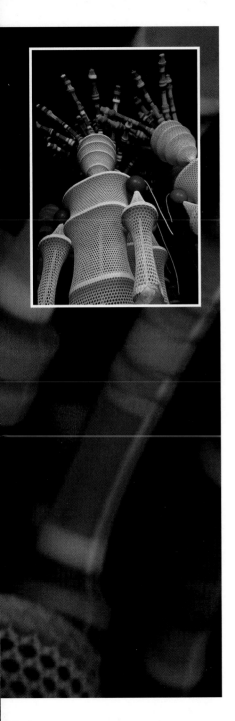

"With every puppet I've used netting so that the wind can pass through, which I like because it also means I can get light passing through too," says Curry. "A lot of these are not puppets as we usually think of them. They aren't manipulated by the wrist and fingers; they are body puppets, so when you move your legs the puppet responds. When you do something that's choreographed, the puppet responds. In their way, the puppets are very much like costumes—they react to your own body movements."

Curry's regal creations are sufficiently complicated that 30 assistants are required to help each puppeteer get into costume. It's a process similar to "suiting up scuba divers or astronauts." The costumes also need to be lightweight—they weigh from eight to eighteen pounds—both for the safety of the puppeteers and for the ability to make the performance seem light and effortless. The performers have to carry and manipulate the puppets for the entire show, and they're also backstage rushing around to get ready. As a result, Curry designed the suits to feel natural, "like a suit you enjoy wearing."

Curry says he's made friends with the huge winds in Epcot®. "These big, light structures gather a lot of wind, animating the puppets and making them even more beautiful. After all, if it were only stuntmen holding up big objects, there would be no performance.

The humorous and gangly Disc Man
puppets, left and inset, are made of soft
foam discs covered by a nylon mesh shell.

The puppets have to be really uplifting and light and seeming like they're having a good time."

Now that he has met the challenges, Curry says he is delighted with the Epcot® show. "I like the intimacy of having an audience right here. I believe in Epcot and find the park ideal for a big live performance that reinforces what Epcot represents. When you design for Disney, you can realize your full dream. We're doing something here that only Disney can do."

"A lot of these are not puppets as we usually think of them.**"**

Michael Curry,
Puppet Designer

Curry, opposite right, and his crew assemble the agile, futuristic Hammered Man puppets in a warehouse in St. Helens, Oregon. In all, he designed forty different puppets and built three of each. All the puppets incorporate the performer in their design: nothing is hidden from the audience.

Curry and his team referred to the sketch shown at middle far left during the construction of the Sprite. A crewmember, left, stretches featherweight netting over a flexible frame.

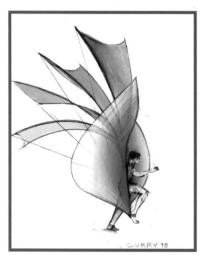

CURRY 98

Neat rows of Disc Man puppets await the trip from the Oregon warehouse to Epcot® World Showcase. It took a crew of fifty nearly a year to create all of the puppets used in *Tapestry of Nations*.

Bold headpieces for the Aztec Man puppets await shipment to Epcot® World Showcase.

A practice session in suiting up takes place before the Sprite leaves the Oregon warehouse. The complex costume must be able to withstand the wear and tear of two daily performances, as well as heat, humidity, and Florida's bright sunlight.

> **❝I enjoy the absolute immediacy of an audience three feet away in broad daylight looking you in the eyes.❞**
>
> *Michael Curry,*
> *Puppet Designer*

Great walking sculptures, the giant puppets fill World Showcase Promenade with a fun-filled cavalcade of imaginative shapes, colors, and textures.

T raveling along with the puppeteers and performers in the *Tapestry of Nations* procession are the giant rolling percussion units, or Millennium Clocks, designed by Lynn Holloway. They are the only set pieces in *Tapestry of Nations.*

"These Millennium Clocks are born of several influences and capture a vision of both the past and future," he says. The large wheel was inspired by an antique astrolabe not unlike the one Columbus used to measure the latitude on his voyages of discovery. A collection of marine compasses used by the great explorers of the second millennium provided inspiration for design details and timeworn finishes. The hammered "metal" band, incised with Roman numerals, suggests an astronomical

The Millennium Clocks

THE ROLLING PERCUSSION UNITS TAKE SHAPE

Scenic designer Lynn Holloway, above, created the rolling Millennium Clocks that are the only set pieces in *Tapestry of Nations*. Opposite page, one of his intricate sketches of the giant clocks.

clock dating from the mid-1500s. Set between the spokes of the large wheel, clusters of drums represent the tribes and nations. Beating not unlike the human heart, these drums resonate with the pulse of time passing, calling mankind to dance and celebration. Wheel covers represent both the sun and the moon, which order the days. The clock is topped with a jeweled finial pronouncing the dawn of the new millennium and showering light on the faces of all who gather for our celebration.

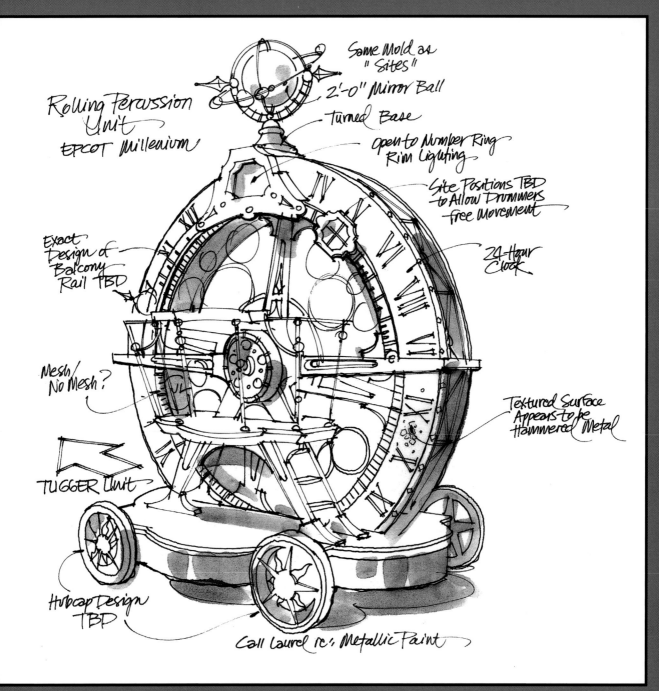

The Millennium Clocks are a symbolic representation of the passage of time. They both recall our past history and move us toward future possibilities. "Note the hours moving forward on the port side of the clock, while traveling backward on the starboard side. The sense should be that these ancient/modern timepieces are used ceremoniously to mark the passage of time every thousand years."

From inception, the designs for the Millennium Clock incorporated details from historic timepieces, as Holloway's early concept sketches show.

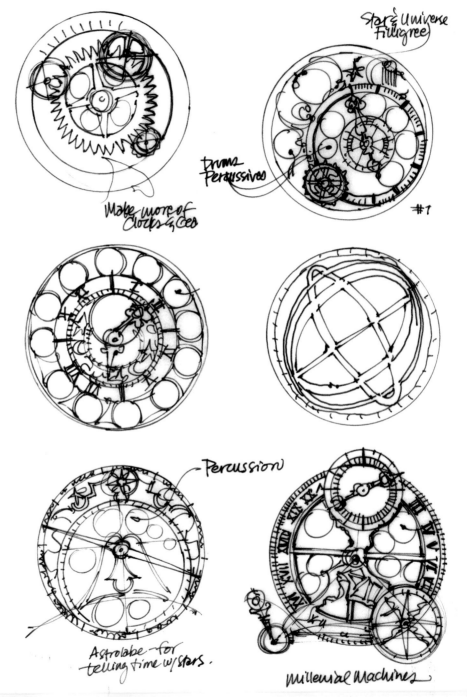

Drum Faces

French Astrological Clock

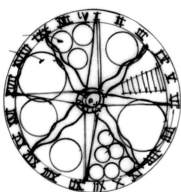

Simple Equinoctial

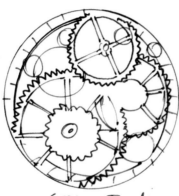

Gears on Parade

Drumheads become design element

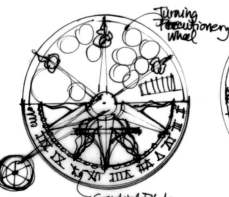

Turning Executioners Wheel

Sundial Plate Remains Plumb — hangs from Pivot

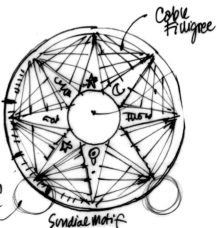

Cable Filigree

Wheel rests & turns in cradle

Sundial Motif

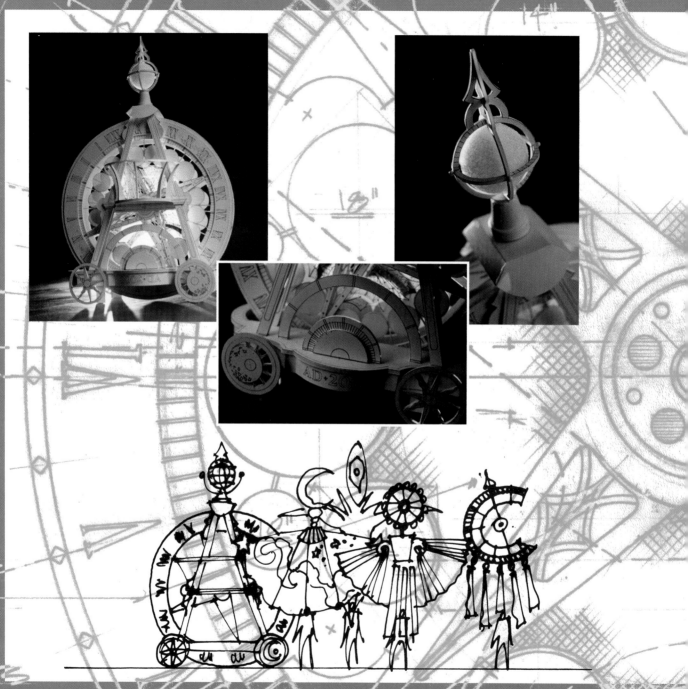

From the first meeting, the greatest challenge facing the creators of *Tapestry of Nations* was to figure out what it means to celebrate the millennium, and Holloway's clocks were the answer: a dynamic visual statement connecting the past, present, and future. Initially Holloway wanted giant circles that could roll along the World Showcase Promenade, but for guests' safety the clocks were anchored with smaller wheels—"training wheels," Holloway calls them—as shown in the scale models on the opposite page. The clocks were designed to be in proportion with the *Tapestry of Nations* puppets, as these early sketches illustrate.

Nearly 19 feet tall and 16 feet long, the Millennium Clocks were handcrafted at the Walt Disney World® Central Shops. Below, metal is welded into the perfect circles that will support the drumheads on the face of each clock.

There are 15 Millennium Clocks in *Tapestry of Nations*. Also known as rolling percussion units, each clock incorporates remarkable details including a variety of drumheads. During the performance, drummers, one standing on the raised platform on each side of the clock, beat out the rhythm for the procession.

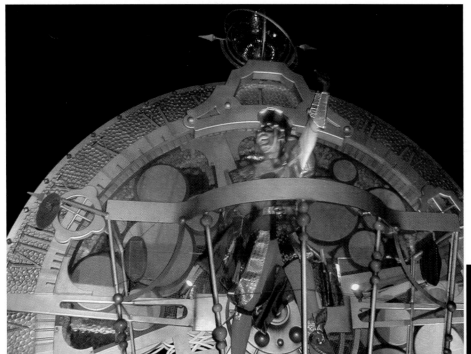

As the Millennium Clocks wind their way around the World Showcase Promenade, 30 drummers pound out the heartbeat of the celebration.

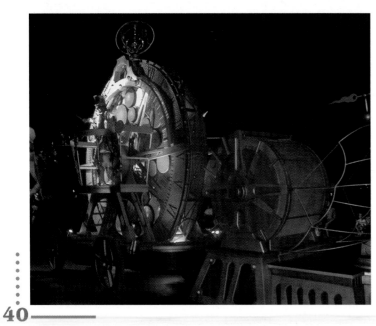

Tapestry of Nations is a procession with no decorative floats, so the costumes must make a strong visual statement. It was the job of costume designer Marilyn Sotto Erdmann to create the attire for all of the performers, including the mystical, stilt-walking Sage of Time.

Sotto Erdmann has a rich history in the film business that began in the mailroom at MGM Studios, delivering mail to Clark Gable, Judy Garland, Mickey Rooney, "all the big stars, directors, and producers," she recalls. After art school, Sotto Erdmann started sketching and designing for major productions including *The Ten Commandments, Around the World in Eighty Days, Spartacus,* and *Man of a Thousand Faces.* Charlton Heston,

Creative Costuming

AN IMAGINATIVE BLEND OF ART, FUNCTION

Tapestry of Nations costume designer Marilyn Sotto Erdmann, above, started her career in Hollywood sketching and designing for major film productions like *The Ten Commandments.* Opposite page, a close look at the rich fabrics and motifs used for the Sage of Time costume.

Yul Brenner, Frank Sinatra, Dean Martin, and Ann-Margret are among stars she has designed for, working in consultation with such designers as Helen Rose and Edith Head.

Sotto Erdmann's first designs for Disney were costumes for Disneyland Paris in 1988. In the years following she created costumes for nearly all the company's major theme parks. This experience was excellent preparation for *Tapestry of Nations,* allowing a natural marriage between her flamboyant designs and the realities of the heat and humidity in Florida. "The fabric for the costumes is state-of-the-art, breathable microfiber," explains Sotto

Erdmann. "We constantly research and test new materials."

For the puppeteers' costumes, Sotto Erdmann worked with puppet designer Michael Curry to complement the color and design of each puppet. The outer-space galaxies displayed on the costumes for the Sprites who interact with Epcot® guests were created by transferring real photos to the costume fabric. The fabric for the drummer costumes consists of blocks and shapes in subdued colors, an "almost Elizabethan look."

The Sage of Time is "all brilliance and sparkles" in a palette of iridescent bronze, gold, and copper—"all the metal colors because that is the fruit of the earth," explains Sotto Erdmann. She used symbols of alchemy "with philosophic and magical associations" on the flowing robes, alluding to the belief in the Middle Ages that alchemists had miraculous, transformative powers.

Sotto Erdmann's early drawings for the Sage of Time, opposite page and above, depict an imposing and regal figure, majestic enough to open the entire celebration. She designed the headdress to represent the sun, an icon familiar to all cultures. The symbols decorating the flowing cloak allude to the medieval belief in the transformative power of alchemy. At right, a preliminary sketch of the drummers' costume, inspired by the Elizabethan period.

As Sotto Erdmann refined her drawings, the costume designs underwent subtle changes—a more celestial look for the Sage of Time's headdress, opposite page, a more primal look for the drummer's attire, below. At right, her sketch for the puppeteers' costume. Although the designs borrow from myriad historic fashions and styles, contemporary fabrics and state-of-the-art construction were used to ensure the performers would be as cool and comfortable as possible.

A close look at the golden Sage of Time headdress, below. At right, an animated puppeteer shows off her finished costume. Sotto Erdmann worked with Michael Curry to make sure her costumes worked with the color and design of the puppets.

The Sage of Time is "all brilliance and sparkles" as he makes his grand entrance for *Tapestry of Nations*. The majestic effect is literally heightened by the performer's stilts, which, combined with the Sage's elaborate robes, can make traversing World Showcase Promenade a challenge.

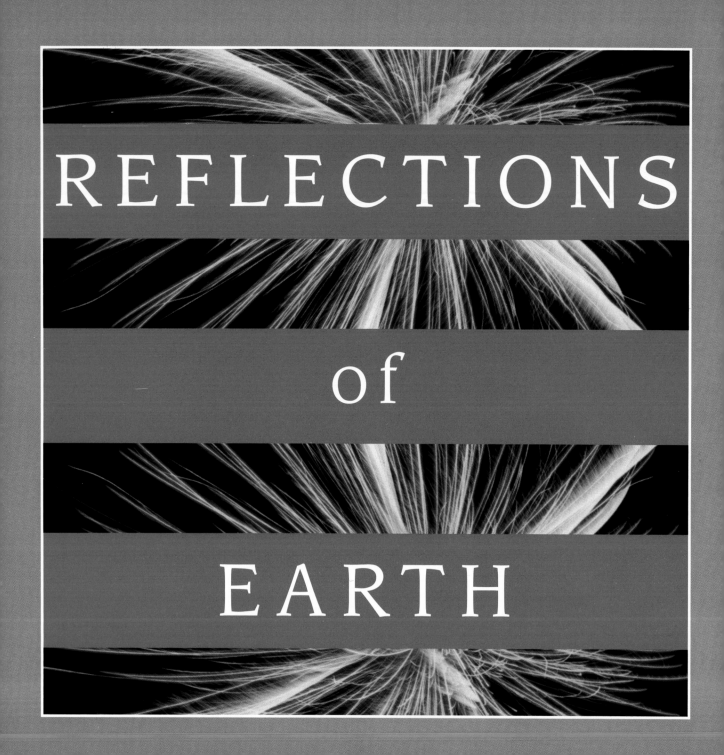

REFLECTIONS

of

EARTH

Every day we're alive on the planet is special. Every morning brings a new opportunity, a chance to move forward, to experience new things, to better ourselves, to grow together as people. In *Reflections of Earth,* not only are we looking back at our history and our planet, but we are reflecting on the things that we have done and how far we've come. And we have to contemplate the future, we have to realize that we are responsible for making each day as bright and as promising as we can.

— Don Dorsey, creator and show director of *IllumiNations 2000: Reflections of Earth*

Incredible new fireworks, opposite page, play an integral role in *IllumiNations 2000: Reflections of Earth*, the unforgettable nighttime show at Epcot®.

T wenty-seven-foot-tall torches arrayed around the lagoon are lit, and a mystical, musical wind quiets the audience. A sage, grandfatherly voice invites all to gather around for a storytelling in honor of this time of transition: the story of our home, planet Earth, and the link between past and future. As if blowing out a candle, the sound of a breath extinguishes the torches, leaving the audience in darkness. A heavy drumbeat begins, accelerating faster and faster, culminating in a thunderous roar.

Thus begins *IllumiNations 2000: Reflections of Earth*, the sensational music-and-fireworks finale to each evening of the 15-month-long Epcot® Millennium Celebration. Don Dorsey, the show's director,

IllumiNations 2000

THE GRAND FINALE OF EACH DAY

IllumiNations 2000: Reflections of Earth show director Don Dorsey, above, says his goal was to use this unique millennial celebration to remind people that our home planet is an amazing place. Opposite page, an early rendering depicts the finale, with the Earth Globe opening to reveal a giant torch rising 40 feet into the air.

has created and directed more than half a dozen nighttime shows on the World Showcase Lagoon, as well as the popular synthesizer arrangements for Disney's classic Main Street Electrical Parade. But according to him, *Reflections of Earth* is "the ultimate," an unbeatable combination of music, state-of-the-art pyrotechnic effects, and an emotional history of planet Earth. In *Reflections of Earth,* Dorsey hopes to give his audience a highly charged emotional experience, so that when guests look back on the millennium they will remember something special.

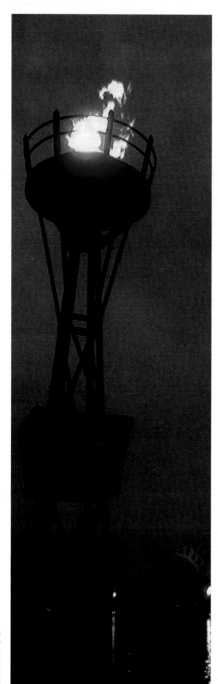

A Play in Three Acts

Though the audience may only perceive an unsurpassed display of pyrotechnics, Don Dorsey has meticulously constructed the nighttime show as a three-act play, with music serving as the central, binding element.

Composer Gavin Greenaway took Dorsey's show outline and timing framework and created musical themes for each act. The music, Dorsey felt, was the key to the show, the backbone of the entire experience. The musical composition Greenaway created overwhelmed Dorsey. "The first time I heard the music," he recalls, "I was actually moved to tears."

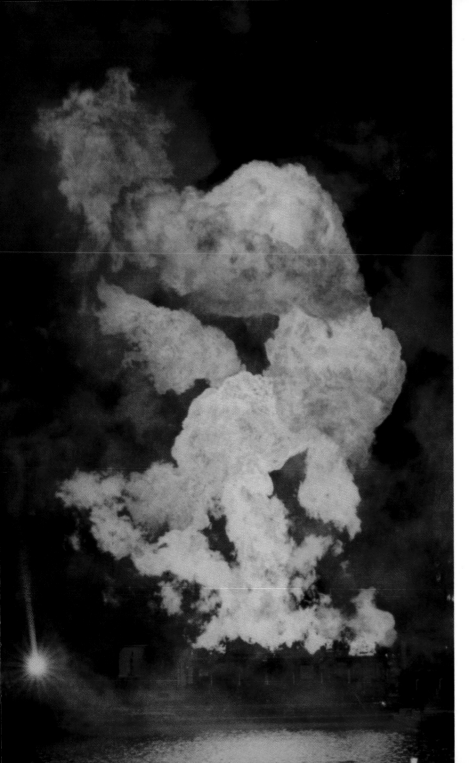

Act I, "Chaos," captures the tumultuous, fiery early history of the planet Earth. It's the perfect showcase for spectacular effects: a shooting star explodes over the center of the lagoon; dancing fire and fountains shoot up like jets of lava; balls and plumes of fire erupt into the air, then veer off in all directions, while lasers produce eerie effects overhead in what Dorsey calls "a frantic ballet of fire and pyrotechnic chaos."

Act II introduces symbolic "Order." The Earth Globe, a 28-foot-high LED video system wrapped around a sphere, floats to the center of the lagoon amid the sounds and cries of animals and birds. Lush green vegetation appears and slowly evolves on the massive video screen. Hundreds of images inspired by the history of the Earth swirl to life: animals, primitive man, exploration, natural beauty, architectural wonders, and famous faces from history are among the sequences that pass over the surface of the Earth Globe. The pace of the images accelerates in tandem with the tempo of the music and fireworks, as tailed comets leap into the air, showering the globe with "pixie dust." The final image is of an astronaut, who sees the Earth in its true context: as one place, home to all people.

"Meaning" is the theme of the celebratory Act III, which brings the story of our planet up
to the present day. Uplifting music, lasers, lights, animated fountains, and a barrage of
fireworks contribute to this intense finale. As a single voice swells to a chorus, the Earth
Globe blossoms, opening from the top like the petals of a flower. In the center of the
unfolding Earth, a flaming torch rises slowly, heralding the dawn of the new millennium.
The music crescendos to a majestic finish and the water and sky are filled with fireworks
unlike any seen before. Then, after a moment's breath, a final acceleration of the
drumbeat is heard beneath a huge barrage of fireworks. "The sound of the explosion
is tremendous," says Dorsey, "finally leaving all in silence."

The Fireworks Guy

To complement the original and powerful musical score, Dorsey hoped to integrate breathtaking visual effects into the show. "One of the challenges was to take a step back from what had gone before and imagine new effects that could help us tell our story."

Disney hired world-class fireworks designer Eric Tucker, whose fiery creations have garnered international acclaim. Tucker has worked on everything from the Rolling Stones' *Bridges to Babylon World Tour* (1997-1998) to numerous Super Bowl halftime extravaganzas. He has won gold and silver awards at the Benson and Hedges International Fireworks Competition, considered the pinnacle of pyrotechnic competitions.

Dorsey challenged Tucker to devise new and innovative pyrotechnics, to create effects never before attempted. For example, he asked Tucker to create a field of stars in the lagoon that would ignite, burn for a period of time, then change color and continue to burn. In pursuit of their vision, Dorsey and Tucker traveled to China, where they met with a fireworks manufacturer and actually invented the star field effect they visualized.

Dorsey also collaborated with Walt Disney Imagineering and Walt Disney World® Creative Entertainment to create a technology that launches fireworks shells with compressed air. An electronic chip rides along with the shell, allowing pyrotechnics experts to control the height of the shell's flight before it bursts. Using this technology, shells may be exploded at precisely the right instant, Dorsey explains, "so our timing capabilities are 100-fold better than any of the traditional fireworks shows."

Left, fireworks designer Eric Tucker in China, where he worked with local manufacturers to invent new colors and effects for *Reflections of Earth*. Right, Eric and Bernie Durgin (fireworks production manager), are given a tour of a fireworks factory by Jim Shih, son of the owner.

Standing beneath a statue of Lee Wen, the inventor of fireworks, from left to right: Kevin Smith, purchasing manager; Bernie Durgin, fireworks production manager; Don Dorsey, show director; Steve Zimmerman, producer; John Shih, factory owner; and Eric Tucker.

Though *Tapestry of Nations* and *IllumiNations 2000: Reflections of Earth* are two entirely different creations, the thread of continuity is the powerful and expressive music of composer Gavin Greenaway.

"I'm tying the whole thing together with the music, because the shows are very different," says Greenaway. "*Reflections of Earth* is an adventure, a discovery of life, while *Tapestry of Nations* communicates a feeling of oneness, of belonging, with many cultures and people together."

Known for his great musical versatility, Greenaway's work has been showcased in commercials, film, television, and other artistic

The Music

CREATING HARMONY WITH TWO DIVERSE SHOWS

"When it comes to music, I feel I can say something that I can't say any other way," says composer Gavin Greenaway. Opposite, a sheet from Greenaway's score for *Reflections of Earth*. Following pages, Greenaway composed the music for both *Tapestry of Nations* and *Reflections of Earth*, contributing the rhythmic backbone to a combined multimedia experience consisting of giant puppets, state-of-the-art fireworks, and the singular visual grandeur of the Earth Globe.

ventures. Nothing, however, presented quite the challenge of creating the two Epcot® shows from scratch.

"For a couple of weeks, I was nowhere. It was quite a puzzle," recalls Greenaway. Early on, he collaborated with his business associate and friend Hans Zimmer, the Academy Award®–winning composer of the score to Disney's *The Lion King*.

In the beginning the two shows were not thematically tied, and Greenaway was working only on the music for *Reflections of Earth*. He studied the storyboards and script with show director Don Dorsey, and then set to work on a piece expressing the creation of the Earth. "It's the whole history of our planet in a quarter of an hour," Greenaway says with a smile.

REFLECTIONS OF EARTH

Greenaway worked hard to write music that would blend seamlessly with the show's visual effects. Most fireworks displays, he explains, use familiar classical music spliced together in segments of 30 or 40 seconds. While the immediate impression can be satisfying, the end result often doesn't have a thread. The challenge in *Reflections of Earth* was to create an original sound with smooth transitions "so that when you come to the end you feel like you've experienced an incredible symphony choreographed to a light show."

For *Tapestry of Nations*, the musical introduction had to be bold in order to set the mood for the elaborate procession. "Each time I wrote a theme," recounts Greenaway, "I would think 'It's okay but it's not grand.' And so I built on that, writing something stronger each time. I ended up writing something huge—but I would never have gotten to this magnitude immediately."

The music was recorded at Abbey Road in London, with musicians from the Royal Philharmonic and the London Symphony Orchestra, and a 30-member chorus. Greenaway invented a new "language" for the chorus to sing—chants that mean nothing but sound like words. The ethnic origins of the "language" are deliberately indeterminate. "It's gentle-sounding," its creator explains, "so wherever you come from it means whatever you want it to mean."

The music, too, does not fit any specific genre. "You'll hear entrances of great composers, but also tunes you might hear on ballads in the Top 40. There's a range of influences, a broad spectrum of sound, that makes the music very accessible."

Greenaway hopes that when guests leave, they will be humming one or two of the tunes. "I hope they'll be a bit more neighborly as they go home, and feel that it was a good communal experience."

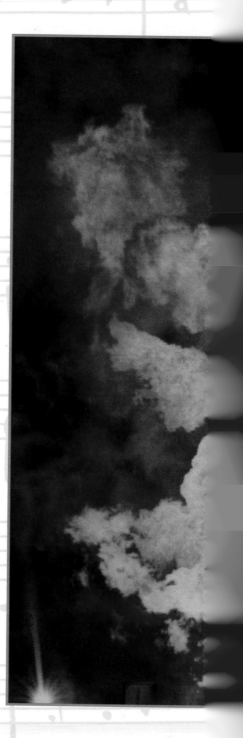

For Dorsey, the high-tech, rotating Earth Globe is "the real thrill, a centerpiece that is truly meaningful."

The 350-ton barge on which the globe is mounted is the most complicated piece of show equipment ever built by Walt Disney Imagineering.

The 28-foot-diameter globe rests on a 10-foot pedestal and contains the world's first spherical LED video system. Thousands of tiny "pixels" are planted into the round surface at key angles, horizontal to the water and directed toward the guests. These pixels carry the visual images that sweep across the surface of the Earth Globe.

The Real Thrill

WHIRLWIND TRIP THROUGH TIME ON A GIANT SPINNING GLOBE

The steel-ribbed Earth Globe, above, doubles as a three-story video screen that projects vivid images during *Reflections of Earth*. Opposite page, workers are dwarfed by the 28-foot-diameter globe, which rotates on a 350-ton floating island housing six computer processors, 258 strobe lights, and an infrared guidance system.

The earth is hollow and peels open during the finale, like flower petals, to reveal a large "eternal flame." The gas torch is on a column that lifts 38 feet into the air; the burner is in the shape of a donut so that fireworks can launch from the center of the flame.

Nearly 300 images telling the story of planet Earth flash on the Earth Globe throughout *Reflections of Earth*. Recognizable geographic scenes include the Himalayas, Victoria Falls, and the coast of Ireland; architectural pieces include the Statue of Liberty, Mount Rushmore, the Sydney Opera House, and the Golden Gate Bridge. Thousands of images were considered for the emotional, whirlwind trip through time.

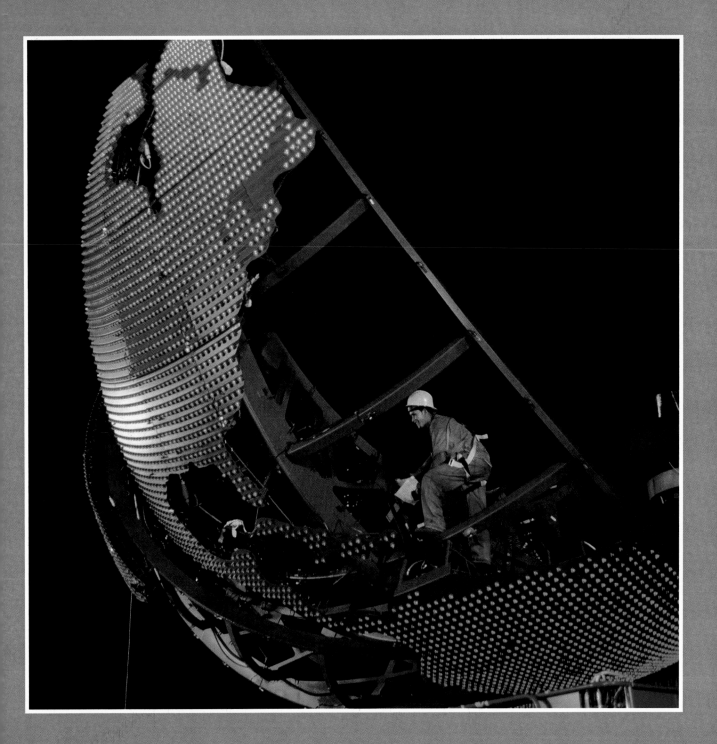

Reflections of Earth is truly a feast for the senses. Complementing Gavin Greenaway's dramatic score and the thrilling sights and sounds of the fireworks designed by Eric Tucker and Don Dorsey is the visual splendor of the 28-foot-high Earth Globe. More than 300 images illustrating the history of the Earth float across its LED surface during the performance.

SHARING

the

CELEBRATION

The vision behind the Epcot® Millennium Celebration is of a world without boundaries, a space to be shared. In the Millennium Village, for example, each of the countries contributing exhibits and interactive displays seeks to share with our guests the richness of their history, the vitality and accomplishments of their present, and their future promise. To accommodate this expansive conception, we strove to create a truly global community, one encompassing the sights and sounds of a diversity of nations.

—Terry Dobson, senior show designer for Millennium Village

Opposite page, a montage of Epcot® guests who have left a personal record of their millennium memories at *Leave A Legacy*. This dramatic work of art was created by Walt Disney Imagineering and installed at the entrance to Epcot.

To create Millennium Village—the gigantic new pavilion in World Showcase—the team of Walt Disney Imagineers and Epcot cast members turned into modern-day explorers as they traveled around the globe searching for exciting "gifts to the world" to share with Epcot® guests.

"This village of countries gives Epcot guests a richer experience and reinforces that this event, this moment, includes the entire world," says Orrin Shively, senior show director for Epcot.

Traveling around the world allowed the team to translate their discoveries into a fascinating and informative series of shows for Millennium Village visitors. Countries with interactive exhibits include

Millennium Village

GIFTS FROM AROUND THE WORLD

Terry Dobson of Walt Disney Imagineering, above, helped steer the creation of Millennium Village. Dobson visited countries around the world looking for the best stories to share with Epcot® guests. Opposite page, an early rendering of the new World Showcase Pavilion's exterior.

Brazil, Saudi Arabia, Israel, Sweden, Scotland, Chile, Denmark, and the emerging country of Eritrea, which used to be part of Ethiopia.

Having no interior walls, the 60,000-square-foot pavilion is truly a world without borders. In Brazil visitors can play a virtual soccer game, or take a walk through the Amazon rain forest. In the Chile exhibit, guests get a close-up look at the mysterious Moai statues from Easter Island, and observe the work of Chilean scientists who are catching fog and turning it into drinking water. Israel has a simulator attraction that takes guests through centuries of Jerusalem's history, then highlights modern miracles created by Israeli companies and organizations.

Terry Dobson, senior show designer for the project, explains that Eritrea was the only country in the pavilion he didn't visit, because the tiny nation was at war. The Millennium Village team hopes that by bringing this little-known country to Epcot®, guests will witness firsthand the importance of cultural diversity. "Although this country has been fighting for its independence for the last 15 years, it has been around since the dawn of history," says Dobson. "It is a role model for the rest of the world, with nine tribes that thrive and live as one." A traditional Eritrean coffee ceremony, hosted by a native, is the country's way of sharing its gifts in Millennium Village.

Dobson and his team found that several nations are sensitive to misconceptions about their international identity and are eager to portray their lands in a more positive light. "We courted many countries, did designs for many, and, like a snowball, the momentum built," he says proudly. Along the way, Millennium Village partnered with the United Nations and the World Bank, and consulted with the planners of Hannover Expo 2000 to present stories of humanitarian projects taking place around the world.

According to George Kalogridis, vice president for Epcot, travel and sensitive negotiations were only part of the initial challenges. Once they agreed on the countries to be represented, Kalogridis's team was responsible for hiring—and providing housing for— more than 300 new cast members from around the globe.

> **Everyone has an opportunity to become a contributor to this wonderful soup of world culture.**
>
> *Terry Dobson,*
> *Senior Show Designer*

Early rendering depicts the Millennium Village pre-show that introduces guests to ambassadors from eight countries who tell about their homelands. Right, the pavilion interior is "a world without borders," allowing guests to step from one country to the next. This drawing shows the giant egg-shaped chambers that immerse guests in Sweden's four beautiful seasons of the year.

A Walk Through the Pavilion

The self-paced trip through Millennium Village is intended to be socially interactive, continuing a tradition that Walt Disney started with the theme park—creating a family space that can be shared by everyone.

In the pre-show, the experience starts with video stories from the Hannover Expo 2000. Ambassadors in traditional costumes from eight countries—Ethiopia, New Zealand, Indonesia, South Africa, Namibia, Kenya, India, and Israel—welcome guests and share their country's "gifts to the world." Ethiopia's gift, for instance, is agriculture, which was introduced there 5,000 years ago. Kenya tells the story of a women's co-op that makes fabrics and sells them to create schools, hospitals, and roads in their village. All eight share stories of hope for a better future.

Spread throughout the U-shaped pavilion are the eight

major exhibits—Brazil, Saudi Arabia, Israel, Sweden, Scotland, Chile, Denmark, and Eritrea—highlighting each country's gifts through song, dance, architecture, art, and innovative projects.

Whether a guest wants to spend only a few minutes or several hours, the major exhibits offer something of interest for just about everyone. Visitors can hit a few golf balls in Scotland, step into three-story-high egg-shaped chambers in Sweden to experience the four seasons, or explore the high-tech Web pages of an Internet Family Scrapbook in Saudi Arabia.

The intimate Millennium Village Artisans' Community offers traditional crafts, everything from pottery and weaving from Venezuela to vine crafts from Thailand. Egypt, South Korea, Peru, Greece, Lebanon, and Sri Lanka are among the other countries with craftsmen working in the Artisans' Community.

"All of these experiences and activities, high tech and low tech, offer a vehicle for bringing people together to provide a lasting impression," says Dobson. "We want guests to take their time, experience the richness at their own rate, and stay as long as they want."

The final stop in Millennium Village is the Gifts to the World Game, which allows guests to test their knowledge. According to Dobson, "Games are ubiquitous to every culture around the world and transcend any language barrier."

As the game concludes and other attractions beckon, the Millennium Village planners hope that guests are left wondering what their own gift to the world should be. "Everyone," Dobson insists, "has an opportunity to become a contributor to this wonderful soup of world culture."

Above, ambassadors from around the world mingle with guests in the Millennium Village pre-show. In the center of the spacious room, video monitors tell stories of exhibits developed in conjunction with Expo 2000 Hannover, the international exposition to take place in Hannover, Germany, from June 1 to October 31, 2000. Top right, guests can play golf in Scotland or score a goal in a virtual soccer game in Brazil, neighbors in the 60,000-square-foot pavilion. Right, interactive games teach guests about Saudi Arabia's fascinating history.

Millennium Ambassadors

Throughout Millennium Village, cultural representatives from around the globe share heartwarming stories of their homelands. Dozens of the young ambassadors are participating in the 15-month-long Walt Disney World® Millennium Celebration, eager to learn about America and one another's cultures while they are here, and eager to share stories of faraway places with Epcot® guests.

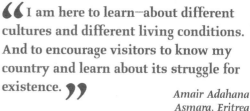

This is a dream come true—to meet people from different countries and to learn about their cultures. America is cool!

Katy Mendes
Sao Paulo, Brazil

I am here to learn—about different cultures and different living conditions. And to encourage visitors to know my country and learn about its struggle for existence.

Amair Adahana
Asmara, Eritrea

Everything is so big here in America! Life seems easier here, friendlier ... Americans are not so serious as the Swedes.

Erika Magnusson
Stockholm, Sweden

66 I come from a beautiful country, the world's friendliest island. If you meet someone on the street, they will invite you home for dinner. **99**

Sharon Mason
Bridgetown, Barbados

66 We are all here sharing and learning to work together for the same purpose. I'd like others to know that the people in Israel are very warmhearted. **99**

Guy Levy
Jerusalem, Israel

66 Chileans are very warm, friendly, and open. We try to always look forward, to maintain strong relations with other countries. **99**

Cristobal Corro
Santiago, Chile

> ❝ I want to rid myself of the stereotypes of other countries. I'm learning and making lasting friendships. ❞
>
> *Mindy File*
> *Pocahontas, Illinois*

> ❝ People are laid back at home—here everyone is in such a rush! I'd like to share more about my country: we're at peace, the war is behind us, and we're looking toward the future. ❞
>
> *Nikola Glavan*
> *Vela Luka, Croatia*

> ❝ The toughest adjustment? Keeping time. In Africa, we never keep time. And people here are straight to the point, unlike my culture where we beat around the bush. ❞
>
> *Mercy Mbugua*
> *Nairobi, Kenya*

66 The best part about being here is the teamwork and inter-cultural sharing. I'm learning to be more open-minded. **99**

Ibrahem Al-Haidari
Riyadh, Saudi Arabia

66 There are so many new faces and new friendships! My country is so small—it's fun to meet friendly people from so many different cultures. **99**

Ira Murah
Bali, Indonesia

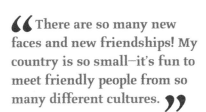

"Learning about other cultures and countries is quite fascinating! You learn that your way is not necessarily the right way."

Neil Graham
Kinross, Scotland

"This is a great opportunity to learn about the lives of people from other countries and to share my own culture with them."

Ereth Rodriguez
Queretaro, Mexico

"Life seems so easy here. There is more freedom and people are more outspoken."

Thomas Liebenberg
Pretoria, South Africa

“ Meeting all these people has been the greatest thing about coming here. When we return home, the friendships will remain with us. ”

Dawit a Rumicho
Addis Ababa, Ethiopia

“ In India, one doesn't talk to strangers, and life is very crowded. Here it's very friendly, with big roads and open spaces. ”

Navneet Hayer
New Delhi, India

83

World ShowPlace Theater

Diane Rinkes is buried in videotapes. Stacks and stacks of the black plastic boxes are piled high on her desk backstage at Epcot®. As the entertainment manager for the Millennium Celebration, Rinkes spends hours every day previewing the work of hundreds of musicians, singers, and dancers who hope to perform in World ShowPlace, the 250-seat theater in Millennium Village.

"Scheduling is my life," says Rinkes with a wry smile. Part of her job is to sort through the videos—solicited and unsolicited—to come up with enough talent for World ShowPlace for every day of the 15-month-long celebration. While letters were sent to tourism boards in many major countries, Rinkes says some of the most fascinating entertainers are from unfamiliar, exotic places like Fiji, Sri Lanka, Malta, and the Turks and Caicos Islands. In fact, one country was so small she had never even heard of it.

Among the first performers to be signed for a long-term commitment were puppeteers from Denmark's Tivoli Gardens, who bring to life the tales of Hans Christian Andersen.

Each group performs for at least one week, although most stay for ten days. Once the performers have been chosen, it is Rinkes's job to make sure they all have performance visas and room reservations. After they arrive, she schedules their show times, and arranges transportation and meals. No detail is too small—even dietary restrictions are part of her copious notes.

In spite of the manic pace and minutiae, Rinkes wouldn't trade places with anyone else. "I have learned a tremendous amount about our world and met some of the nicest and most interesting people on earth," she says. "We have so much to learn from other cultures."

Entertainers from around the globe will perform in Millennium Village's World ShowPlace Theater throughout the 15-month-long Epcot Millennium Celebration. They include (1) Living Legends—Native American, Polynesian, and Latin performers from Brigham Young University; (2) Mechola Jerusalem Dance Troupe, Israel; (3) Areyto, Ballet Folklorico Oficial de Puerto Rico; (4) SamulNori Hanullim, Korea—featuring Mr. Kim Duk Soo, artistic director; (5) Ballet Folklorico Español "Carmen Cantero" y Grupo de Coros y Danzas Mazantini, Spain; (6) The Bayanihan, the Philippine National Folk Dance Company; and (7) Living Legends, Brigham Young University.

"It was the special genius of Walt Disney to take spaces and make them unique," says John Hench, senior vice president of design for Walt Disney Imagineering. Now 89 years old, Hench started in the Disney Story Department in 1939 and was an artist for *Fantasia, Cinderella, Alice in Wonderland,* and other Disney films. He went on to help design and build Walt Disney's dream called Disneyland. And he was the original art director for Epcot® and the chief designer of Spaceship Earth.

Today, the master Imagineering artist is nurturing the next generation of talent by passing along his expertise. For the Millennium Celebration, Hench and a team of young Imagineers

Leave A Legacy

GIFTS FROM AROUND THE WORLD

Master artist John Hench, above, led the Walt Disney Imagineering team that designed the *Leave A Legacy* sculptures near the entrance to Epcot®. Opposite page, an early rendering of the sculpted and polished granite megaliths, covered with engraved images of guests who have visited Epcot during the Millennium Celebration.

designed *Leave A Legacy,* an artistic tribute to the millennium landscaped into the Epcot entryway.

Leave A Legacy creates a new threshold for Epcot: sculpted granite megaliths appear to emerge out of the ground like foothills, continuing to grow as they point up toward Spaceship Earth.

"Walt thought every inch of the place should be part of the story, and he maintained that thresholds, or entranceways, played an especially important role," explains Hench. "The megaliths are pointing in the same direction and at the same pitch as the legs of Spaceship Earth so that they create a sense of movement by leaning into the spaceship, adding more warmth and more

presence by appearing to cradle Spaceship Earth."

A closer look at the granite stones, which range from 3 feet to 19 feet high, reveals surfaces that are covered with 1-inch-square metallic tiles, etched with images of Epcot® guests who are commemorating their crossing into the new millennium. There is room for 750,000 of these steel-etched images on the *Leave A Legacy* megaliths, which were designed to create a portrait of today's diverse world.

To accomplish this mosaic of images, guest photos are digitally captured on clear acetate sheets, then applied to

Justin Jorgensen 10.12.98

Early ideas from the Walt Disney
Imagineering team for *Leave A Legacy*. The
sketch, above, shows how the megaliths follow
the same pitch as the giant legs that support
Spaceship Earth.

Right, a computer-generated drawing shows how the granite stones appear to emerge out of the ground like foothills, cradling Spaceship Earth. Below and opposite page, a "before and after" look at the transformation of Spaceship Earth and the Epcot® entryway.

" I think the instinct to leave your mark is strong in everybody. "

— John Hench, Walt Disney Imagineering

a steel plate and acid-etched for posterity in less than 48 hours. Once an engraved image is affixed to a stone, the photo can be located on computers at the site. Certificates indicating tile locations are mailed to guests. Guests can further personalize their millennial commemoration by visiting Disney Online's *Leave A Legacy* Web site at www.Disney.com/Living Legacy, where they can build a living family tree that can blossom over time.

According to Hench, the *Leave A Legacy* threshold is unique, one of those experiences you won't find anywhere else in the world.

Epcot® guests pose at *Leave A Legacy* picture booths, left. The photos are processed on the computer, below.

Images are digitally captured on clear acetate sheets, then applied to a steel plate and acid-etched in less than 48 hours, above. About four days after photos are taken, "memory tiles" are affixed to the *Leave A Legacy* sculptures, right. Until the panel is complete, a picture representation of each tile is on display in the Legacy Gallery near Spaceship Earth.

Left, guests find their photos on the *Leave A Legacy* sculptures. Locator cards are issued as photos are taken, and once guests return home, they receive a certificate with their image and its exact location on the sculptures. With the location address, guests, family, and friends can quickly find the image.

For the first time in the history of the Walt Disney World® resort, guests can interact with an attraction at the park *after* they go home. Images from *Leave A Legacy* are posted at www.Disney.com/Living Legacy. Once guests are on line, they can record hopes and goals for the future, add their own digital photographs, and create a living family tree.

The Icon

Rising 240 feet, the icon for the Epcot® Millennium Celebration is Spaceship Earth, visible from above on airplanes arriving in Orlando, and on all horizons for miles beyond the theme park.

For the 15-month-long celebration, Walt Disney Imagineering decorated the world's largest geosphere with the gloved hand of Mickey Mouse from the "Sorcerer's Apprentice" segment of the Disney film *Fantasia,* symbolically sprinkling the sphere with a light show of pixie dust.

> **"The wand is about everything we do—the magic of the moment, a moment that could only happen at Disney."**
>
> *— Orrin Shively,*
> *Walt Disney Imagineering*

The Disney team wanted a spectacular visual statement about greeting the new millennium with a hopeful attitude. A dozen Walt Disney Imagineers labored to create the playful design. Mickey's arm and familiar three-fingered glove stand 8 stories high, and his wand is 116 feet long, sprinkling more than 150 stars, ranging from 3 to 6 feet in height. The sculptural "2000" follows the curve of Spaceship Earth.

"This design draws on the heritage of Imagineering," says Orrin Shively, senior show director for Epcot®. "The wand is about everything we do— the magic of the moment, a moment that could only happen at Disney."

It took 6 months to dress up Spaceship Earth for this celebration of a lifetime.